Adventures in Science

by CHARLES D. NEAL

Illustrated by
RALPH E. RICKETTS

WHITMAN PUBLISHING COMPANY
RACINE, WISCONSIN

contents

Library of Congress Catalog Card Number: 63-9471

Copyright © 1963 by Whitman Publishing Company
Printed in the U.S.A. by Western Printing and Lithographing Company

WHAT IS A SCIENTIST?

A scientist is someone who specializes in chemistry, physics, biology, medicine, or in any one of a great number of subjects like these. The word *scientist* comes from the Latin word *scire* which means *to know*. A scientist measures, weighs, and tests until he has the answers to certain questions.

Opinions do not interest the scientist. An opinion is an idea believed to be true. For instance, at one time people believed that animals such as frogs and salamanders grew out of the mud at the bottom of ponds and streams. This was an opinion. Scientists discovered long ago that it was a false opinion. They proved that frogs and salamanders grew from eggs which were laid at the bottom of ponds and streams.

What do I need to become a scientist?

Intelligence and the desire to be a scientist are all you need.

Must I be a genius to become a scientist?

Being a genius is helpful, but it is not necessary. Any average pupil can learn to make a good living and enjoy his work as a scientist.

When should I begin to study science?

Right now! Many noted scientists of today got their start when they were your age.

sound

HOW SOUNDS ARE MADE

Did you know that sounds are really caused by a rapid movement called vibration? Sound is made when an object vibrates, causing the air surrounding it to vibrate.

Strike a tuning fork or a steel table fork against some hard object. The floor will do. Touch it lightly with your finger. Feel the vibrations? You can see the prongs vibrate if you look closely enough. Sound may be made by the vibrating prongs, but too faintly to be heard.

Now strike the fork again. Then stand the handle of the fork on a hard tabletop. Notice that you hear a louder sound when the handle touches the table. The tabletop acts as a sounding board, making the sound louder.

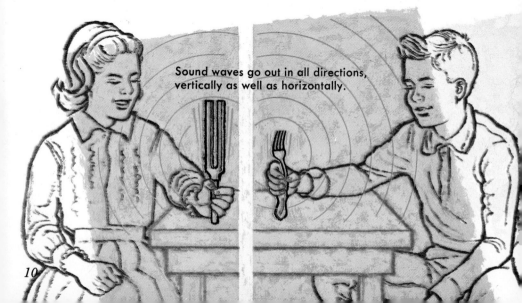

Sound waves go out in all directions, vertically as well as horizontally.

Here are some interesting facts.

When an object vibrates it causes the air around it to vibrate. When this happens sound waves are formed. Sound waves move away from the vibrating object in all directions. If you could see them they would look like the waves caused by dropping a stone into a pan of water. But sound waves cannot be seen.

When sound waves reach you, your eardrums begin to vibrate. These eardrum vibrations are then carried by nerves to the brain where they are understood as sounds.

The ground acts as a sounding board. It makes the lion's roar louder and more frightening.

SOME SOUNDS ARE DIFFERENT FROM OTHERS

Some sounds have a low pitch. Distant thunder is one of these. Other sounds have a high pitch. Have you ever heard the squeaking of a mouse? Pitch means the number of vibrations an object makes per second. The more vibrations, the higher the pitch. That is, a shrill sound is heard. The fewer the vibrations, the lower the pitch. A deep sound is heard. Sounds may also be loud or soft.

Make a frame like the one pictured. Fasten stovepipe wires at one end of the board. Tie one brick to one of the wires; tie four bricks to the other. The second wire, held more tightly across the two wedges, is said to have greater *tension*.

By shortening or lengthening the wires, changing to different kinds, or adding bricks, you will be able to produce many variations in pitch.

Pluck each wire. The sounds from the wire having the greater tension will be higher than sounds from the

B

A

One-Inch
Shingle
Nails

Screw
Eye

Wooden
Wedges

Stove
Pipe
Wire

Bricks
With
Holes

One- by Eight-Inch
Board, Two Feet Long

Pour a little water in a soft drink bottle. Blow across the mouth of the bottle and listen to the tone. Add more water. Blow across the mouth again. You will notice a rise in pitch.

The tension, length, thickness, and material of which its strings are made are what give a violin its tone.

other wire. This proves that the greater the tension, the higher the pitch.

Press the center of one of the strings firmly to the board at A and pluck it at B. The pitch will be higher. Pitch can be raised by making a wire or string shorter.

Fasten an aluminum wire to the board. The wire should be the same size as the stovepipe wire. Tie two bricks to each wire. Pluck the wires. The aluminum wire, being soft, will have the highest pitch. This proves that the lighter the material of a string or wire, the higher its pitch.

Fasten a thicker steel wire to the board, attaching two bricks to this wire. Now pluck the wires. The thinner wire will have a higher pitch than the thicker one. This proves that for a given material, the thinner the wire the higher the pitch.

HOW SOUND TRAVELS

Boats travel through water. Airplanes and rockets travel through air. Sound waves, too, must have something through which to travel.

Scientists tell us that sound is caused by vibration. When sound travels through a substance, the molecules of the substance vibrate rapidly.

Sound waves can travel through gases, through solids, and through liquids. If the air is removed from a space, sound cannot travel in it. Such an empty space is called a vacuum. Sound cannot travel in a vacuum because there are no molecules for the sound waves to set into vibration.

Try this experiment. Remove the tops from two oatmeal boxes and punch a hole in the center of the bottom of each box. Put a piece of string about fifteen feet long through the holes in the boxes. Tie a button to each end of the string to hold it in place. Give one of the boxes to a

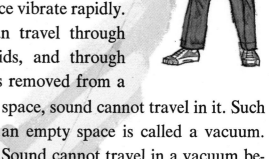

Button   String

Oatmeal Box

SOUND TRAVELS THROUGH WATER

Water is a good conductor of sound. Sometime when you are swimming, have a friend hit two stones together while you are both underwater. You will be surprised at how well you hear the sound.

friend and have him hold it to his ear. Walk away until the string is fairly tight. Speak into your box and your friend will hear what you say. Let him talk to you and you will hear him.

Now try the experiment again. But this time use a small wire such as a stovepipe wire instead of string. Which gives the better results, string or wire? You should have found that the metal wire carried sound waves better than string.

SOUND TRAVELS THROUGH THE GROUND TOO

Put your ear to the ground and listen to distant sounds as the Indians did.

Which is the better sound conductor: water or earth?

Time how long it takes for distant sounds to reach you.

THE SPEED OF SOUND

When you were swimming, have you ever tried to run through the shallow water? Did you find that your movements were slowed down by the water? You move faster on dry land. Sound waves act in just the opposite way. They travel faster through water than through air. Sound waves travel at different speeds through many different substances. The rate of speed depends upon the density or thickness and the elasticity of the substance.

Sound travels more slowly through air than through most substances: a little over a mile in five seconds, or about 1100 feet per second.

Ask a friend to stand at a distance from you, at least two blocks away. He should then make a loud noise—

When sound waves strike a wall or a mountain they bounce back. You may hear an echo. To hear a clear echo, you must stand at least fifty-five feet from a large solid object, like a brick wall or a canyon wall.

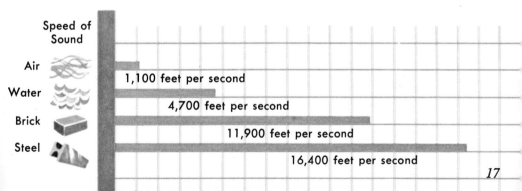

Sound waves travel faster and farther through water than through air. Destroyers use the echo-sounding principle in their sonar systems to locate enemy submarines.

shout, strike a drum, bang two pieces of metal together—so that the sound reaches you. As he makes the noise, he should give a hand signal. When you see the hand signal, begin to count "one thousand one, one thousand two," and so on. It takes one second to say each thousand number. How far can you count before the sound reaches your ear? If you hear the sound before you have time to count, have your friend increase his distance another block or two. Repeat the experiment.

You can try another experiment during a thunderstorm. From the safety of your home, count the seconds between the time you see a flash of lightning and hear the noise of the thunder. Divide the time by five and you will know how many miles you are from the lightning.

Speed of Sound

Air — 1,100 feet per second

Water — 4,700 feet per second

Brick — 11,900 feet per second

Steel — 16,400 feet per second

17

air

HOW AIR TAKES UP SPACE

You say, "We can't see air. Is it a 'something'?" The answer is Yes. Air, made up of many different gases, is all around us. It can be a "something" as gentle as a spring breeze. It can be a "something" of such great force that during hurricanes it completely destroys buildings.

Stuff a piece of newspaper tightly into the bottom of an empty jar. Be sure that it cannot fall out even when the jar is held upside down.

Pour enough water into a bucket to cover the jar. Holding the jar upside down, lower it into the bucket until it is completely underwater. Hold the jar in place for a few moments. Take the jar out of the water and remove the newspaper. You will find that it is dry, even though the jar was covered by water.

Air takes up space. Nothing else can occupy that space at the same time.

1

Crumple a newspaper and push it firmly into a jar.

3

When you take the newspaper out of the jar you will find it completely dry. Water could not enter into a space that was already occupied—and air occupied the space around the newspaper.

2

Hold the jar completely under water.

Suspend your yardstick from a broom or mop handle placed between two chairs of the same height.

AIR HAS WEIGHT

As you breathe air and walk through it you get no hint that it weighs anything. Some people will tell you it has no weight. But they are wrong and you can prove it.

Drill a small hole through the exact center of a yardstick. Also drill a small hole exactly one inch from each end. Run a piece of string through the center hole and hang the yardstick from the string so that it swings freely. You now have a simple scale. Run pieces of string of equal length through each of the end holes in the yardstick and tie them in place. Tie an empty balloon to each string. The yardstick should now hang level. This means that the scale is balanced. If the yardstick is not in perfect balance, add small amounts of chewing gum to the higher end until it hangs level. Now untie one balloon and blow it up. Using the same string, retie the blown-up balloon so that the air cannot escape. Notice that it unbalances the yardstick. Both balloons are the same, but the one hanging lower weighs more because of the air contained in it.

Using a household scale, weigh an empty inner tube. Then pump air into it and weigh it again. You will find that the inner tube weighs more with air in it than it did when empty.

AIR HAS PRESSURE

Put about a pint of water in an empty eight- or ten-quart oilcan. Make sure the can does not leak and that the top is open. For the sake of safety the opening must always remain open when a can is being heated.

Place the can over a stove burner and heat it until steam comes from the opening. Using a heavy pair of gloves remove the can from the stove to the floor. Quickly close the opening with the screw cap. Make sure that the cork or gasket is in place on the inside of the cap. This is necessary because the can must be airtight for the experiment to work. Watch the can carefully. In a short time it will collapse as though crumpled by a giant hand.

See what air pressure can do. Be sure to wear heavy gloves or to use pot holders while doing this experiment.

1
Add
Water

2
Heat

3
Put Cap
on Can

Here is what happened. At the beginning of the experiment air pressure was equal inside and outside the can. But by the time you screwed the cap tightly to the opening, the steam had forced most of the air out of the can. Then as the water in the can cooled, the steam condensed; that is, it

Filling station attendants use an air gauge to check the air pressure in automobile tires.

changed back into water. But the water took up less space inside the can than the steam. Since the can was tightly sealed, air could not enter to fill the space left by the cooling condensing steam. The pressure on the outside of the can thus became greater than the pressure on the inside. At last the can collapsed.

4 Can
Crumples

heat

ONE WAY IN WHICH HEAT TRAVELS

Did you know that heat is motion? You may ask, "What moves?" Molecules move. All matter—water, iron, wood, gas—is made of molecules, particles too small for the eye to see. But they do move, even in material as hard as a piece of steel. Moving molecules create energy which is given off in the form of heat. The faster they move, the greater the heat. Since everything is made up of molecules, everything has heat.

Heat travels in one of three ways: by conduction, by convection, or by radiation. To find out how heat travels by conduction, do the following experiment.

1

After you have dripped wax on the metal rod, let it cool before continuing the experiment.

2

Using a lighted candle, drip eight balls of wax onto an old metal curtain rod. Space them about two inches apart. Then, using a heavy glove, hold the curtain rod in such a way that you can heat the end close to the wax balls with a candle. Notice that the first wax ball to melt is the one nearest the flame. As the heat travels from molecule to molecule down the curtain rod, the other balls will in turn melt. Do not be surprised, though, if the last few balls do not melt. Much of the heat may be lost by radiation and the far end of the rod may not get hot enough to melt the wax.

Here is another example of heat traveling by conduction. Heat from the burner causes the molecules in the bottom of the skillet to vibrate very fast. These in turn cause the molecules next to them to begin to vibrate. Finally all of the molecules in the skillet, even those at the outermost edge, are vibrating. At last the handle becomes too hot to touch.

HEAT ALSO TRAVELS BY CONVECTION

Place a thermometer on the floor for a few minutes. What is the temperature? Next place the thermometer somewhere in the room as close to the ceiling as possible. Leave it there for a while. When you read it again you will find that air near the ceiling is several degrees warmer than air near the floor. This is true even though heat may be coming from ducts near the floor. Warm air always rises. Heat moving in this way is said to travel by convection.

To see how convection works, light a candle and stick it to a plate with a few drops of wax. Cut both ends from a tall juice can and place it over the candle as a lamp

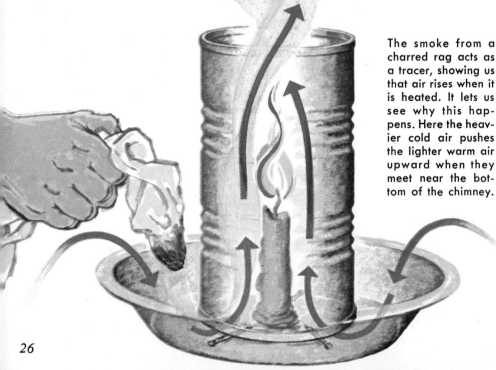

The smoke from a charred rag acts as a tracer, showing us that air rises when it is heated. It lets us see why this happens. Here the heavier cold air pushes the lighter warm air upward when they meet near the bottom of the chimney.

Heating by convection is found in every kitchen. As the water near the bottom of a pan is heated, it expands, becomes less dense, and rises to the top. This process is repeated until soon all the water is heated.

chimney. Hold the bottom of the chimney away from the plate with three small number 6 finishing nails. Light a small piece of rag and blow out the flame. The rag will glow and continue to give off smoke. Hold the smoking rag near the bottom of the lamp chimney. See how the smoke is drawn in? Then hold the smoking rag above the chimney and watch as the smoke rushes upward.

Warm air expands. As it expands it takes up more room. At the same time it also becomes less dense; that is, it becomes thinner. When heavier cold air meets light warm air, the cold air pushes the warm air upward. An interesting fact is that heat can travel by convection in any liquid or gas.

HEAT TRAVELS BY RADIATION TOO

Hold your hand about an inch below a lighted electric light bulb. Feel the heat? It could not have reached your hand by conduction because the air between your hand and the bulb is a poor conductor. In fact, air is an excellent insulator. Neither could the heat have reached your hand by convection, since heat rises and your hand is held below the light bulb. The heat reached your hand by radiation.

This is how radiation works. The vibrating molecules in a hot object send out electromagnetic waves. These are like light waves, except that the wave lengths are longer. The waves travel 186,000 miles a second, the same as the speed of light. When they strike an object their energy is changed back into heat motion of the molecules in the object. Another interesting fact is that radiation heat waves can be reflected, transmitted, and absorbed by various materials.

Get two shiny tin cans of the same size. Remove the labels from each. Paint one of the cans and its lid black. When the paint has dried, fill each can with water and close the lids. Set the cans out in the sun. A half hour later use a thermometer to record the temperature of the water in each can. Which can of water is warmer?

Dark colors absorb heat waves, light colors reflect them. The water in the black can will be warmer than the water in the unpainted can.

In summer we wear light colors to reflect the sun and keep us cool. In winter we wear dark colors to absorb the rays and keep us warm.

Heat travels from the sun to the earth by radiation. Electromagnetic rays from the sun are changed back into heat when the rays strike objects on the earth.

HEAT WAVES ARE:

A. Reflected

B. Transmitted

C. Absorbed

light

HOW LIGHT IS REFLECTED

Few of us give much thought to the light that is all around us. Yet it is one of the most puzzling of scientific subjects.

Light is a kind of radiant energy. It travels in a straight line through the air at a speed of 186,000 miles per second.

You can easily see how light is reflected by trying a simple experiment.

Stand at one side of a mirror. Have a friend stand the same distance from the other side of the mirror. Hold a newspaper in such a way that he cannot see what you are doing. Beam a flashlight directly toward the center of the mirror at the eye level of your friend. Ask him what he sees when he looks toward the mirror. He should see the reflected light beam, but not the flashlight itself.

Direct Light

Reflected Light

Direct light, light of incidence, falls on the subject when you take a picture. But reflected light from the subject strikes the film when the shutter is released.

Angle of Incidence

Angle of Reflection

The angle of reflection is equal to the angle of incidence.

The light shining from your flashlight to the mirror is called direct light or light of incidence. As you might guess, the light reaching your friend's eyes is called reflected light.

Here is an interesting fact. Light shining directly on an object forms an angle of reflection. These two angles are the same. That is, they always contain the same number of degrees.

LIGHT IS MADE OF MANY COLORS

You learned on page 10 that sound travels in waves. Light also travels in waves. But these waves are only about 1/50,000 inch long. That is, they are about 1/1000 as long as the width of a horse hair. Even though light waves are small, the waves vary in length for the different colors.

Try this experiment on a sunshiny day. Place a small mirror at an angle in a water glass. Pour enough water into the glass to cover the mirror. Place the glass on a table or chair near a window so that direct sunlight hits the mirror when the window shade is pulled nearly to the sill. Turn the glass slowly until a rainbow forms on one of the walls. Notice the colors: red, orange, yellow,

The rainbow you see through a waterfall or during a rainstorm is a form of spectrum caused by the rays of the sun being reflected through drops of water.

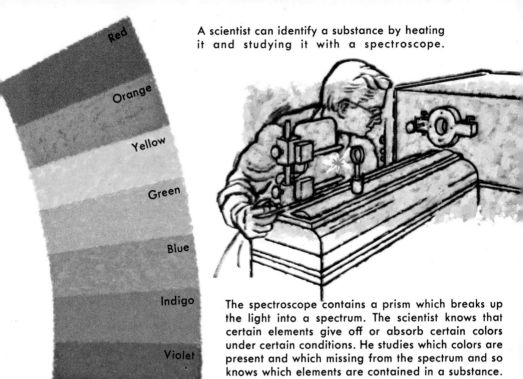

Red

Orange

Yellow

Green

Blue

Indigo

Violet

A scientist can identify a substance by heating it and studying it with a spectroscope.

The spectroscope contains a prism which breaks up the light into a spectrum. The scientist knows that certain elements give off or absorb certain colors under certain conditions. He studies which colors are present and which missing from the spectrum and so knows which elements are contained in a substance.

green, blue, indigo, and violet. The colors in a rainbow always appear in this order. You can remember their names and the order if you think of the name Roy G. Biv. Scientists call these colors a spectrum. What causes them?

Light bends, forming an angle, when it passes from one substance through another of different density. The two substances here are air and water. Violet has the shortest waves and bends the most. Red has the longest waves and bends the least. Because of this difference in the way light bends, each color leaves the substance at a different place. Thus the separate colors of the rainbow are formed on the wall.

HOW LIGHT IS TRANSMITTED

If light passes directly through an object, the object is said to be *transparent*. If light is partly blocked by an object, the object is said to be *translucent*. If light is completely blocked by an object, the object is said to be *opaque*. This easy experiment will show you how light is transmitted.

Place a lighted flashlight on a table. Look at it through a piece of clean glass. Notice that the light readily passes through the glass. The glass is transparent.

GLASS
Transparent

Now look at the lighted flashlight through a piece of waxed paper. Some light gets through, but the image is blurred. The waxed paper is translucent.

WOOD
Opaque

WAXED PAPER
Translucent

Since light rays do not pass through the hand, a shadow is cast when the hand is placed in front of the flashlight.

Next hold a book or a piece of cardboard between your eye and the lighted flashlight and a piece of white paper. A shadow will form on the paper because light rays do not pass through an opaque object. In this experiment you have also proved that light travels in a straight line.

Transparent materials are used in packaging today, allowing us to see what we are buying.

electricity

HOW TO MAKE STATIC ELECTRICITY

If you were to ask a scientist to tell you about electricity, he would probably answer, "Electricity is a matter of electrons. The movement of these electrons is a current of electricity." Among other things he would probably tell you that Benjamin Franklin was one of America's earliest experimenters in the field of electricity. For thousands of years before Franklin's time man knew of electricity in such forms as lightning and the shock felt in holding an electric eel.

On a cold, dry day, put on woolen clothing and slide back and forth a couple of times across the seat of an

Experiments with static electricity work best when the air is cool and dry.

automobile. Then touch a metal part of the automobile body with your hand. Feel the shock? Slide back and forth across the car seat again. This time instead of touching a metal part of the automobile body shake hands with a friend. Notice him jump? You gave him a charge of static electricity.

The effects of static electricity can be seen when you pick up bits of paper with a hard rubber comb, or when your hair stands up as you comb it.

You can achieve the same effect by rubbing your feet on a woolen rug and touching a doorknob or a person.

Place a few torn bits of newspaper on a table. Run a hard rubber comb through your hair a few times. Then place the comb close to the bits of paper. Notice how the comb attracts the pieces of paper. Again run the comb through your hair several times. Then hold the comb above your hair. Notice how the hair streams upward to meet it. The comb acquired a charge of static electricity which caused the bits of paper and your hair to act as they did.

Lightning is caused by static electricity generated in the clouds.

NEGATIVE AND POSITIVE CHARGES

Early scientists learned that there were two kinds of electricity. Benjamin Franklin called these *negative electricity* and *positive electricity*.

Electrify a hard rubber comb as explained in the last experiment. Hang it by a piece of thread about ten inches long so that it can swing freely. Electrify a second comb, hanging it in such a way that the two combs can touch each other. Notice them move apart? Both combs are negatively charged and so they repel each other. In the same way, when two or more objects are positively charged they repel each other. Like electric charges always repel each other.

Like Electric
Charges
Repel

Unlike Electric
Charges
Attract

To test for negative
and positive charges,
hang combs from the
end of a workbench
so they swing free.

Again electrify a hard rubber comb and hang it as above. Electrify a clear smooth water glass by rubbing it with a piece of silk. Then hold the water glass close to the comb. Notice that the comb is attracted to the glass. The comb is negatively charged while the water glass is positively charged. When one object has a negative charge and another object has a positive charge, they attract each other. Unlike charges always attract each other.

ONE USE OF ELECTRICITY

The first long-distance communication known to man was the telegraph. You can make a telegraph.

Follow the sketch step by step as you work. Begin by making the sounder. Nail a block of two-by-four to a piece of one-inch board. Screw a piece of metal T strip, about two inches wide at the T by four inches long, to the wood block. Use a file to smooth all rough edges. Then drive two box 6 nails into the board so that their heads will be slightly below the T strip.

Make the key by cutting a strip of copper or brass about one inch by five inches long. Bend one end into an L shape. Shape and screw the opposite end to the board and fasten a small roundheaded brass screw to the board directly underneath the key L.

When the key is pushed down, the circuit is completed. The wire-wound nails become electromagnets, pulling the sounder to them with the clicks you hear as you send coded messages.

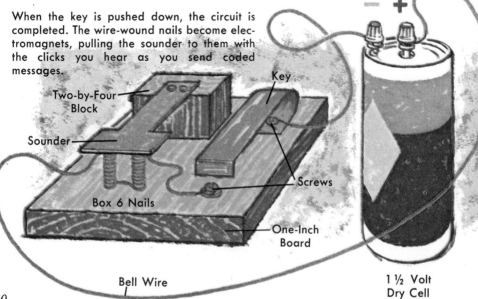

Key

Two-by-Four Block

Sounder

Screws

Box 6 Nails

One-Inch Board

Bell Wire

1 ½ Volt Dry Cell

Remove the insulation from the ends of a piece of bell wire. Connect one end to one of the screws holding the key in place. Connect the opposite end to the center terminal of the dry cell. Be sure that the screws are fastened tightly. Remove the insulation from the ends of a second piece of bell wire. Fasten one

Electromagnets similar to the one you just made are helpful to man in many ways.

end to the screw underneath the key L. Then wind the wire several clockwise turns around the first box 6 nail and the same number of turns counterclockwise around the second. When you connect the wire to the second dry cell terminal your set will be ready to use.

Make another telegraph. Connect it to the same dry cell, as shown here. Then you will be able to receive as well as send messages.

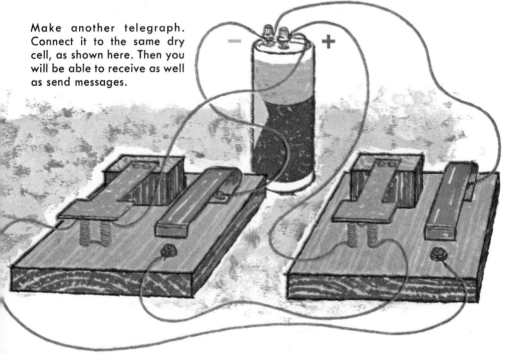

machines

HOW THE INCLINED PLANE WORKS

A cave man, one day in the dim past, stood at the bottom of a hill looking at a big rock. He wanted the rock on top of the hill. At last he picked it up and began carrying it up the steep slope. But it was hard work, climbing the hill carrying that rock. Then the cave man thought of something. He put down the rock and began rolling it upward. It was much easier that way. And so it was, perhaps, that the use of the inclined plane was discovered.

The inclined plane is really a simple machine. To learn how it works, put a small box on the floor near a table. Fill it with four or five bricks. Place a smooth board from the floor to the table. Push the box of bricks up the board to the table. Then replace the board with a slightly shorter board. Again push the box up the board to the table. Which method was easier?

The inclined plane was one of our earliest machines. It permits us to trade force for distance.

Try lifting the box of bricks to the table. Does this require more force than using the inclined plane, or less?

Here are some interesting facts. The inclined plane permits a worker to trade distance for force: the longer the inclined plane, the more gentle the slope and the easier the job. When the distance is increased the amount of force required is decreased. But the total amount of work required is the same.

Many tools make use of the inclined plane. The threads of a screw form an inclined plane.

This man cannot lift the refrigerator directly from the ground to the truck. The inclined plane helps him to do the job more easily.

A wedge is made up of two inclined planes, as are many other cutting tools such as knives and chisels.

HOW WHEELS AND AXLES WORK

Like the inclined plane, no one knows who invented the wheel and axle. Probably some cave man found that large objects could be moved more easily by placing a small log as a roller underneath them. From this labor-saving device, he most likely hit upon the idea of cutting two small sections from his roller log and putting an axle through them. Perhaps the next step of this imaginative cave man was the making of a two-wheel cart. Since then man has used the wheel and axle in many ways.

Make a wheel and axle assembly as shown in the sketch. If you cannot get properly sized dowel sticks from your lumber dealer, shape them yourself from a scrap board of soft wood. Fasten an empty wooden spool to the axle with a small brad so both will turn without slipping. Use screws or small nails to fasten the remainder of the assembly together. Fasten one end of a fishing cord to the spool with a small brad. Tie the opposite end to a small bucket containing three or four bricks. Lift the bucket with the crank handle. Now lift it directly. Which is easier?

Lifting heavy objects with a wheel and axle requires much less force than lifting them directly.

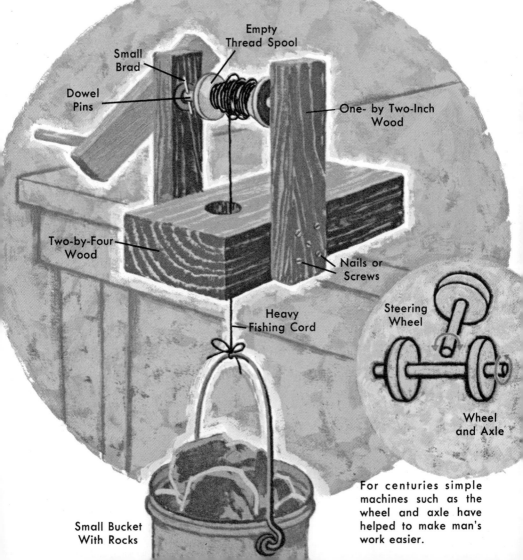

Empty
Thread Spool

Small
Brad

Dowel
Pins

One- by Two-Inch
Wood

Two-by-Four
Wood

Nails or
Screws

Steering
Wheel

Wheel
and Axle

Heavy
Fishing Cord

Small Bucket
With Rocks

For centuries simple machines such as the wheel and axle have helped to make man's work easier.

DIFFERENT KINDS OF LEVERS
AND HOW THEY WORK

Levers are simple machines. They may be straight or bent pieces of strong material, such as wood or iron. The kinds of levers can be identified by the location of three important points: the fulcrum, the weight or resistance, and the force.

For the following three experiments, you will need a one-inch by four-inch by three-foot board, a wedge made from a scrap piece of two-by-four, and a heavy object such as a standard eight-inch building block.

First of all, try lifting the concrete block directly. Then arrange the parts of the lever and the concrete block as shown in the first sketch. Lift the block by pressing down at different points between the end of the lever and the fulcrum. Notice that the farther away from the fulcrum you push down, the easier it is to lift the block. Repeat the experiment twice, arranging the lever and the block as shown and applying force.

For the third experiment, you will need to substitute a bolt run through a stake driven into the ground for the fulcrum.

Perhaps you have concluded that the use of any class of lever makes it easier to lift a heavy object than to lift it directly.

plants

HOW OSMOSIS TAKES PLACE

What goes on unnoticed, taken for granted in plant and animal life, often is a most involved scientific process. Osmosis is one of these things. This is the process by which water and minerals are absorbed by the root hairs of plants. It is also the process by which we absorb digested food into our blood streams. The following experiment shows how osmosis works. Follow each step carefully, exactly as described.

Chip the shell from one end of a fresh egg, being careful not to break the membrane or white tissue just inside the shell. The opening should be about the size of a nickel. Make a hole about the size of a lead pencil in the opposite end of the egg. Place a transparent soda straw into the hole, being careful not to break the yolk. Seal the opening around the straw tightly with drippings from a

When two solutions are separated by a thin membrane the more concentrated solution will pass through, providing the membrane is the kind that will allow it to pass.

lighted candle. Place the egg in a small glass full of water as shown in the sketch.

After two or three hours examine the egg. You will find that some of the egg white has moved up inside the transparent straw. Even though you did not break the membrane at the bottom of the egg, water has passed through it and into the egg. This pushed some of the egg white up into the straw.

An exchange takes place when certain animal or plant membranes have solution on both sides. The membrane allows some material to pass through it, but keeps others out. This kind of exchange is called osmosis. Without it we could not live.

Plants make the green coloring called chlorophyll in their leaves. With the aid of sunlight chlorophyll makes food for the plant from the water and minerals taken in by the root hairs. This process is called photosynthesis.

HOW PLANTS GET WATER

In the last experiment you found out that plants use water and minerals taken from the ground by root hairs. Since roots normally form underground, it is difficult to study their growth. However, in this experiment you will see exactly how plants develop their root systems and how these roots seek out water.

Put about one inch of water into a water glass. Line it with wet blotting paper. Place three or four mustard, radish, or bean seeds which have been soaked in water overnight between the blotting paper and the glass. Set the glass in a warm place for several days. Be sure there

Because they grow toward a water supply, roots can clog a clay sewer pipe. They will enter the smallest hole in a drain tile and in a short time completely fill it with roots.

is some water in the glass at all times. Notice what happens? The first roots to form send out root hairs to help absorb moisture. Without water the plants would soon die.

When the roots are about an inch long, change their position so they point upward, away from the water. Look at them again in a few days. What has happened? Yes, the roots will have begun to turn and grow toward the water supply.

1

2

3

4

HOW LIGHT AFFECTS PLANTS

Plant a few radish, turnip, or bean seeds in two tin cans filled with moist dirt. Water them daily.

Cut a small window in one end of a cardboard box. Be sure no light enters the box except through this window. When the plants in the tin cans are three or four inches tall, place one of the cans in the cardboard box. Examine the plants daily. After four or five days you will find that the plants are growing toward the lighted window. Just as a plant's roots seek water by growing toward a water supply, so its leaves seek light by growing toward a window. When house plants receive light only from one window they should be turned daily to prevent one-sided growth.

Leaves of plants grow toward sunlight in the same way roots grow toward water.

Fold strips of black paper in such a way as to cover several of the leaves of the plant in the second can. Hold the paper in place with paper clips, being careful not to pinch the leaves. Place the plant close to a window. After five or six days remove the paper strips. The leaves will no longer be a bright colorful green. Because they were covered, these leaves will have turned a dull white.

Boards or other objects left lying on the lawn will produce the same effect as the above experiment. Even though a plant receives plenty of food from rich soil and plenty of water, it cannot grow and remain healthy unless it gets plenty of sunlight.

chemistry

AIR IS IMPORTANT TO FIRE

Burning is a chemical process, for when something burns it combines with a gas called oxygen. Oxygen has no color, taste, or odor. It is a gas that makes up about one fifth of the air we breathe. Without it nothing can burn and no plant or animal can live. Here is an interesting experiment that shows how oxygen from the air is used in the burning process.

Use candle wax to fasten a small candle to the bottom of a pan. Pour about an inch of water into the pan. Place a mason jar upside down over the lighted candle. Watch the flame become weaker and weaker. Why does the flame finally go out? Why does the water finally fill about one fifth of the jar?

Many fire extinguishers are filled with carbon dioxide mixed with a soapy liquid. This gas is heavier than air. The soapy liquid foams, holding the carbon dioxide where it is directed. Oxygen from the air cannot reach the flame. Soon the fire goes out.

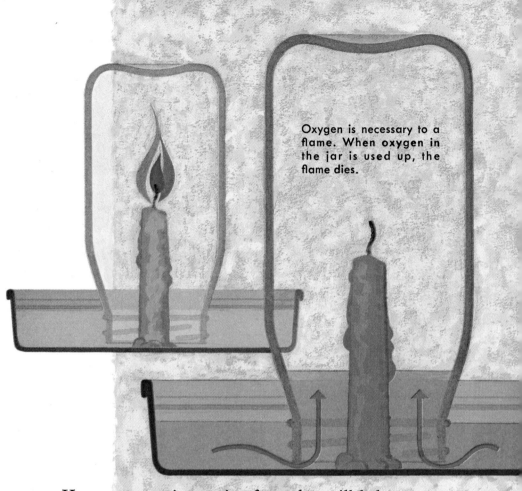

Oxygen is necessary to a flame. When oxygen in the jar is used up, the flame dies.

Here are some interesting facts that will help answer these two questions. Fires need oxygen in order to burn. The flame went out because the oxygen in the air under the jar was all used up. With the oxygen gone, the air pressure on the inside of the jar became less than that on the outside. Therefore, as the jar cooled, the greater pressure on the outside pushed some water up inside the jar. The water simply replaced the oxygen that was used up.

The rust that forms on toys, tools, and equipment left outdoors is caused by the oxidation of iron.

HOW OXIDATION TAKES PLACE

In the last experiment you learned that when something burns it combines with oxygen. The process of combining oxygen with something is called oxidation. There are ways other than burning in which oxygen can combine with something else. For example, the rusting of steel or iron is a slow process of oxidation. Scientists have found that when a piece of iron is given time to rust completely, the rust will be slightly heavier than the original iron. This difference in weight is due to the weight of the iron combining with the weight of oxygen taken from the air.

When lemon juice is put on paper a chemical change takes place. This causes the lettered areas to have a lower burning temperature than the rest of the paper. When the paper is held near heat the letters char, darken, with less heat than the areas around them. As they darken, they become readable.

THIS SECRET
MESSAGE IS

Would you like to be able to write invisible messages on paper? Squeeze a small amount of lemon juice into a bottle or dish and write a message on a regular sheet of writing paper. Be sure to make good heavy lines. The lemon juice will dry without showing a trace of writing. To read the message, simply hold the paper slightly above a heat source such as a kitchen stove burner. As the places on the paper that came into contact with the lemon juice begin to oxidize, the writing will appear.

HOW HOUSEHOLD BLEACHES WORK

In the last experiment you learned that oxidation can take place without the presence of fire, heat, or smoke. The process of bleaching clothing on washday or the bleaching of cotton goods in a factory makes use of still another kind of oxidation process.

Perhaps your mother uses a household bleach in her laundry. The action of some bleaches depends upon the fact that they furnish oxygen. When this oxygen comes in contact with dyes or impurities, compounds without color are formed. A compound is formed any time two or more elements are joined together. Here oxygen is one element joined with several other elements—the dyes or impurities. The grayish looking clothing then looks perfectly white. Thus, the reason for the bleaching action is quite simple.

Here is an easy experiment that you will want to do.

Stir four or five drops of black or blue writing ink into a half cup of water. The mixture should appear somewhat dark in color. Add a few drops of household bleach and stir it thoroughly. Notice how the liquid quickly loses its color. When the oxygen from the bleach comes into contact with the dye in the ink, oxidation takes place. This causes the mixture to become almost colorless.

Many people think that when oxygen is combined with a substance, flame and smoke always result. This is true in only some cases. You have learned that oxidation can take place without causing flame or smoke. It may even take place in water.

Whitman
Learn About Books

Lots of full-color pictures and on-the-spot photographs

Loaded with fun-to-know facts

Printed in easy-to-read type

Good sturdy bindings

11 TURN TO THE SEA *by Dr. Athelstan Spilhaus*

Learn how men of the past studied the sea, and how men of the present go down into it. Find out about the sea's strange creatures, about underwater mountains and rivers, and how one day we may farm and mine the sea.

12 CAVES AND THEIR MYSTERIES *by James McClurg*

Caves can be "live" or "dead" and can "breathe" in and out. Find out how caves form, and about soda straws, moon milk, and cave "decorations." And find out who explores caves.

13 ENGINES, PROGRESS AND POWER *by Don E. Rogers*

The first engine was a human engine, man. Learn how man found out how to make animals and water and steam work for him. Find out how gasoline engines, diesel engines, and rocket engines work.

14 YOUR BODY *by Harry Swartz, M.D.*

Learn about yourself. Find out about the cells, tissues, and organs that make up your body . . . about how bone grows and can rebuild itself when it breaks . . . and about the glands that control the workings of your body.

Whitman Learn About Books—carefully prepared with the editorial assistance of specialists in many fields.

Whitman
REG. U.S. PAT. OFF.